Grump Lump

by Anita Stasson

Consultant:
Beth Gambro
Reading Specialist
Yorkville, Illinois

Contents

BEARPORT
PUBLISHING

Minneapolis, Minnesota

Grump Lump

Let's rhyme!

Here is a tree **stump**.

The **stump** is at a **dump**.

It is by an
old **pump**.

Look out!
Here comes
a mad **grump**!

The **grump** trips on the **stump**.

He lands with
a big *thump*!

Now, the **grump** has a **lump**.

Key Words in the -ump Family

dump

grump

lump

pump

stump

Other **-ump** Words:
bump, clump, jump

Index

About the Author

Anita Stasson lives in Minnesota. She thinks rhyming is the bee's knees.

Teaching Tips

Before Reading

✔ Introduce rhyming words and the **–ump** word family to readers.

✔ Guide readers on a picture walk through the text by asking them to name the things shown.

✔ Discuss book structure by showing children where text will appear consistently on pages. Highlight the supportive pattern of the book.

During Reading

✔ Encourage readers to read with their finger and point to each word as it is read. Stop periodically to ask children to point to a specific word in the text.

✔ When encountering unknown words, prompt readers with encouraging cues such as:

- **Does that word look like a word you already know?**
- **Does it rhyme with another word you have already read?**

After Reading

✔ Write the key words on index cards.

- **Have readers match them to pictures in the book.**

✔ Ask readers to identify their favorite page in the book. Have them read that page aloud.

✔ Choose an **–ump** word. Ask children to pick a word that rhymes with it.

✔ Ask children to create their own rhymes using **–ump** words. Encourage them to use the same pattern found in the book.

Credits: Cover, © Artiste2d3d/Shutterstock and © Roman Samborskyi/Shutterstock; 2–3, © Artiste2d3d/Shutterstock; 4–5, © Feverpitched/iStock, © Michael Burrell/iStock, and © Artiste2d3d/Shutterstock; 6–7, © Photolris2021/iStock and © aristotoo/iStock; 8–9, © Roman Samborskyi/Shutterstock, © Feverpitched/iStock, and © Michael Burrell/iStock; 10–11, © Andrey_Popov/Shutterstock and © Artiste2d3d/Shutterstock; 12–13, © Roman Samborskyi/Shutterstock; 14–15, © Artiste2d3d/Shutterstock; © Roman Samborskyi/Shutterstock; 16TL, © Feverpitched/iStock and © Michael Burrell/iStock; 16TM, © Roman Samborskyi/Shutterstock; 16BL, © Wi6995/iStock; and 16BR, © Artiste2d3d/Shutterstock.

Bearport Publishing Company Product Development Team
President: Jen Jenson; Director of Product Development: Spencer Brinker; Managing Editor: Allison Juda; Associate Editor: Naomi Reich; Senior Designer: Colin O'Dea; Associate Designer: Elena Klinkner; Associate Designer: Kayla Eggert; Product Development Specialist: Anita Stasson

Library of Congress Cataloging-in-Publication Data is available at www.loc.gov or upon request from the publisher.
ISBN: 979-8-88822-052-8 (hardcover); ISBN: 979-8-88822-247-8 (paperback); ISBN: 979-8-88822-367-3 (ebook)